I Just Don't Like the Sound of NO!

Activity Guide for Teachers

Julia Cook

BOYS TOWN Press®

Boys Town, Nebraska

I Just Don't Like the Sound of NO! Activity Guide for Teachers
Text and Illustrations Copyright © 2012 by Father Flanagan's Boys' Home
ISBN 978-1-934490-27-3

Published by the Boys Town Press
14100 Crawford St.
Boys Town, NE 68010

Cover and inside page design: Anne Hughes

Printed in the United States
10 9 8 7 6 5 4

For a Boys Town Press catalog, call 1-800-282-6657
or visit our website: BoysTownPress.org

Boys Town Press is the publishing division of Boys Town,
a national organization serving children and families.

Tips for Teachers and Counselors

Take the time at the beginning of the school year or semester to proactively teach classroom social skills to your students. A few minutes spent at the start of the day reinforcing one of the skills through a short activity can go a long way to helping you have a classroom focused on learning. You can then spend most of your time teaching instead of disciplining students.

- Do your best to give genuine verbal praise to students whenever they accept "No" for an answer or when they disagree appropriately. When you are first trying to teach these skills, use tangible rewards (see pages 5-9) to reinforce students who are using the skills correctly.

- Teach your students that there is a proper time and place to disagree. Create a gesture that will communicate to them that now is not the time to discuss a disagreement and explain how you will use it in advance. For example, when you are teaching the skill of disagreeing appropriately, tell students that there often is a more appropriate time to disagree and an appointment can be made by the child to voice his or her opinion to you. Tell them if they continue to argue, you may pull down an invisible shade in front of your face and walk away. Or you can hold your hand up in the "stop" position to create a visual boundary for the child. Be thoughtful about when you choose to use the gesture. The sign should work in cutting off arguments, but be sure to let students follow up with you if they want to. They will feel that their opinions will be genuinely heard, at the proper time and place.

- When giving a student a reason for saying "No," be concise and to the point. A long, drawn-out explanation is neither necessary nor productive. You can be brief while validating the child's question by replying, "Thank you for asking, but not right now," or "Thank you for disagreeing appropriately, but we can discuss this later." You can always explain your reasons at a better or more appropriate time when the child is calm or the discussion doesn't interrupt the rest of the class or your lesson, etc.

- When a student disagrees with you appropriately, reward the behavior by actively listening to what he or she is telling you.

Stop and think before automatically saying "No" to a student's request. Especially if an individual student has calmly accepted several "No" answers, make an effort to reward that student by granting the next reasonable request. If children never hear anything but "No," they will struggle in continuing to use this skill consistently.

Say YES to NO Star Board

OBJECTIVE
This is a way to publicly recognize those students in your class who have learned and demonstrated the skills of accepting "No" for an answer and disagreeing appropriately.

Teacher Instructions

1. Create a bulletin board with a heading that says, "Say YES to NO Star Board." Display on or near the board posters or cards that list the steps to the skills of accepting "No" for an answer and disagreeing appropriately from the *I Just Don't Like the Sound of NO!* book.

2. The first time students accept "No" for an answer or disagree appropriately, give them a star to add their name to, decorate, and place on the board. Several different-sized star cutouts are supplied on the accompanying CD-ROM.

3. Students who have created stars get to stick a foil star provided by you on their larger, decorated star every time they demonstrate one of the skills.

REMINDER: Let your students take ownership of this activity by allowing them to create their own stars and place them on the star board.

Ping Pong Ball-a-rama

OBJECTIVE

Encourage all students in the class to learn and use the social skills by having them all work toward a group reward.

Teacher Instructions

1. Each time a student or the class as a group demonstrates "Say Yes to No" behavior, have a student put a ping pong ball into a jar.

2. When the jar is full, allow the class to have a "Say Yes to No" celebration. This could be a popcorn party, extra recess, free daily assignment pass, backwards day, hat day, PJ day, etc.

3. In addition to offering the group reward, use the coupons on the following pages to reward individual students for demonstrating the skills of disagreeing appropriately and accepting "No" for an answer. *(Reward coupons on the CD-ROM are offered in **full color** as well as in black and white!)*

WAY TO GO!
GOOD JOB!
WAY TO GO!

You know how to disagree the right way.

Turn this pass in for…

_____

_____

WAY TO GO!

You've joined RJ's SAY YES TO NO CLUB!

NAME:

YOU CAN ENJOY: ....

....

SIGNED.. DATE ....

CONGRATULATIONS!

You just earned _____ minutes of free time for

!

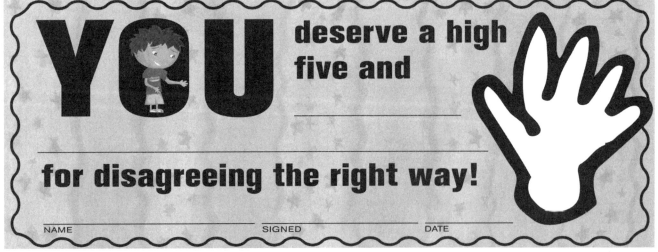

YOU deserve a high five and

_____

_____

for disagreeing the right way!

NAME _____ SIGNED _____ DATE _____

6

Accepting 'No' Reward Coupons

OBJECTIVE
By recognizing students publicly or privately when they demonstrate the skill of accepting "No" for an answer, you increase the likelihood that all of your students will work harder to use that skill in order to enjoy the rewards you offer.

Teacher Instructions

1. When you notice a student accepting a "No" answer from you with a pleasant and cooperative demeanor, try to reward the child immediately by giving him or her one of the privileges below. You may also choose to use another reward that you know will be meaningful to that particular student.

2. This can be done publicly for skills that your class as a whole needs to improve upon. If just that student is struggling with this skill or your students are older, private praise and a reward may be more effective.

3. Remember that verbal praise alone may also be enough to reinforce the behavior you want to see.

4. Below is a list of possible rewards. Ready-made reward coupons that you can copy and use are on the following pages and the accompanying CD-ROM (in color as well as black and white).

- Skip three math problems
- Be first in line for lunch/recess
- Get extra library time
- Get game time in the classroom
- Be awarded free time
- Choose a "helper" job in the classroom
- Get free daily assignment pass
- Use sparkly or other cool pen for assignment
- Receive a 10-Point Bonus Card that can be used in the subject of student's choice
- Choose partner for activity
- Earn a positive note to the principal
- Earn a positive phone call home
- Receive a mini Tootsie Roll
- Get extra computer lab time
- Choose work station
- Earn the use of the teacher's chair for an hour
- Get to have water bottle at desk
- Do half of assignment (e.g., only odd- or even-numbered problems)
- Do schoolwork while sitting on the floor, in beanbag or rocking chair

GREAT JOB!

You know how to

_____

TURN THIS PASS IN FOR:

you were the BEST you can be!

NAME

SIGNED   DATE

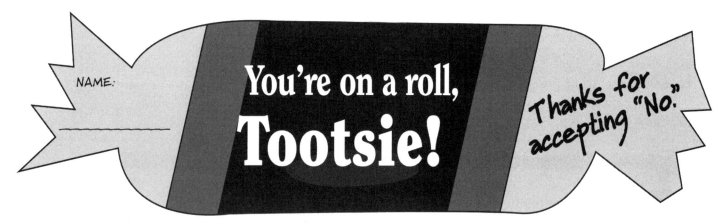

NAME:

_____

You're on a roll, Tootsie!

Thanks for accepting "No."

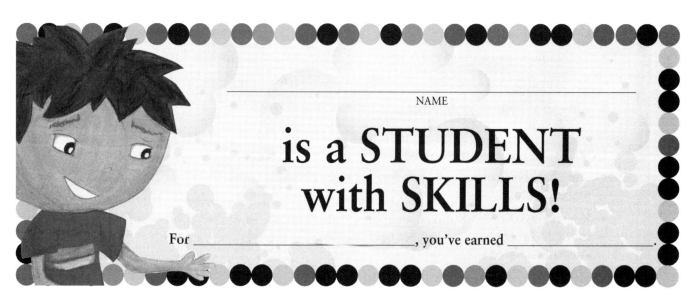

NAME

is a STUDENT with SKILLS!

For _____, you've earned _____.

THANKS FOR STAYING CALM AND NOT ARGUING.
HERE'S YOUR REWARD: _____

_____.

WAY TO GO!

_____
NAME

You demonstrated the skill of _____

_____

and have earned _____.

YOU'VE EARNED:

NAME _____

KNOWS HOW TO SAY "YES TO NO!"

9

'No' Means 'NO'!

Teacher Instructions

1. Have students complete one or both of the *When My Parent Said "No"* and *When My Teacher Said "No"* activity sheets by themselves either in class or as a homework assignment. (Activity sheets are on the CD-ROM. Questions are listed below.)

2. When students have completed the activity, have them gather into groups of four and describe their "No" experiences to each other.

3. Have each group choose one teacher experience and one parent experience and select two speakers to share their stories with the entire class.

ACTIVITY SHEET QUESTIONS

When My Parent Said 'No'

Tell about a time when one of your parents told you "No!" (Use specific details!)

Why do you think you were told "No?"

What did you do? Did you argue or did you accept the "No?"

If you were the parent, would you have said "No" to your request, too? Why or why not?

Would you have handled this situation differently today? Explain.

When My Teacher Said 'No'

Tell about a time when one of your teachers told you "No!" (Use specific details!)

Why do you think you were told "No?"

How did you feel when you were told "No?"

What did you do? Did you argue or did you accept the "No?"

If you were the teacher, would you have said "No" too? Why or why not?

Would you have handled this situation differently today? Explain.

Fit to Be Tied!

Teacher Instructions

Make copies of the *Fit to Be Tied!* activity page on the CD-ROM and distribute to students as an in-class or homework assignment.

After the assignments are completed and turned in, have a class discussion. Ask the students to share what emotions they have felt when told "No." What suggestions do they have about how they might control those emotions in the future?

Face It!

Teacher Instructions

1. Make copies of the *Face It!* activity sheet on the CD-ROM. There are two pages to this activity sheet. Pass out only the first page to students at the start of this activity.

2. When the first drawings are completed, call on a few students to describe the faces they drew. Did most or all of the students draw cranky, angry, unhappy, or disappointed faces? Ask them if this is how they usually feel and respond when they hear the word "No."

3. Have a discussion about the importance of accepting "No" in a cheerful and calm manner. Do they think this is difficult? What thoughts can they have to help them remain positive when they are told "No?" (For example: "If I can accept 'No' with a smile now, maybe later my teacher will be more likely to say 'Yes' to a different request.")

4. Distribute the second page of the activity sheet and have the students answer the questions and redraw their faces.

FACE It!

What does your face look like when you really want to do something or have something but your teacher or parent tells you "No?" Use the blank face below and draw your face.

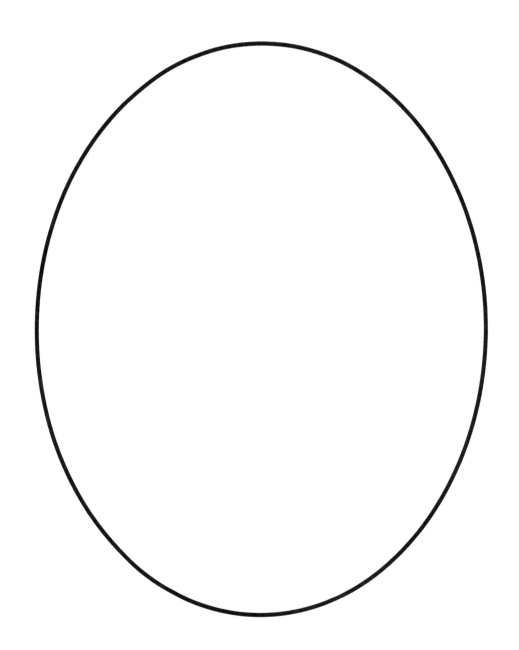

Was your face cranky? Did you draw an angry or disappointed face? _____

_____

_____

_____

Is there a better face to show your parent or teacher when you hear the word "No?"
Draw that face below.

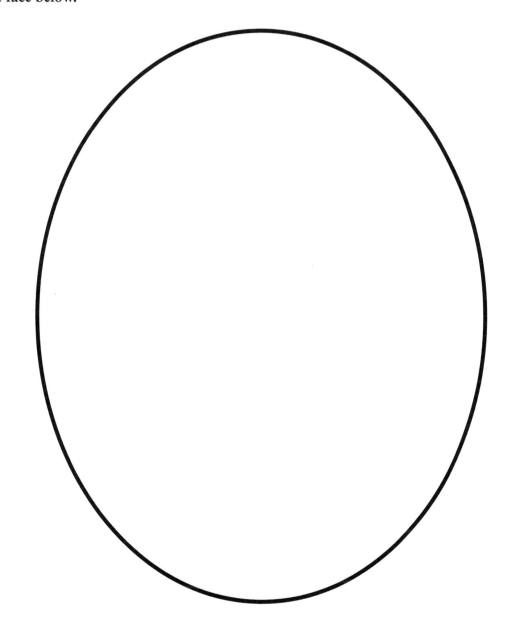

'Gifted'

Materials Needed

- Pair of glasses
- Wooden letters O and K
- Clock
- Notepad with a pen or paperback dictionary

- Magnifying glass
- CD with calming music (sounds of ocean, nature, soft instrumental)
- Something gold with a tag saying "good as gold"
- Plastic costume ears or a set of earphones/headphones

Teacher Instructions

1. Wrap up each item in a decorative package and place in a pile in the front of the classroom.

2. Throughout the day, whenever you see a child using a social skill, particularly accepting "No" for an answer or disagreeing appropriately, allow that student to select one of the packages and set it on his or her desk.

3. Explain in advance that packages should not be opened…they must just sit on the desks until the end of the day. If a package interferes with a student's attention or behavior, the student must return the package to the pile. (With younger students, you may choose to keep the entire activity to a shorter time period.)

4. At the end of the day, divide students into eight groups (three to four students in each), making sure that one package is in each group. Have students open up the presents.

5. Display the steps for "Disagreeing Appropriately" and "Accepting 'No' for an Answer" on the board. Each gift is a symbol for one of the steps.

6. Have groups figure out which step their item represents and have a child with each gift stand up in front of the classroom in the appropriate order as you read over the steps.

7. Items match up to skill steps in this order:

Accepting "No" for an Answer

Pair of glasses:	*Look right at the person who is telling you "No."*
O and K letters:	*Say "Okay" to the person, he's running the show.*
CD:	*Stay calm on the inside and don't disagree.*
Clock:	*You can ask him why later, this is how it should be.*

Disagreeing the Right Way

Magnifying glass:	*Look right at the person when you disagree.*
Something gold:	*Don't scream or use mean words, be the best you can be.*
Notepad and pen or dictionary:	*Tell why you feel differently, give your reasons with facts.*
Ears or headphones:	*Listen closely to what she says, this is how you should act.*

15-Bean Soup

Materials Needed

🐘 Enough bags of dried 15-bean soup so that you can give one bag to each group if your students are divided into teams of four

Teacher Instructions

1. Prior to this activity, secretly pull one-quarter of your students aside and describe the activity to them. They each are to act as a "plant" in their group of three additional students. Explain to them that their job will be to cause some disagreement in their group on how to separate the beans in the bag. Plants should be coached to say "No" (politely) to how others in the group initially want to separate the beans.

2. To begin the activity, split students into teams of four. Give each team a bag of the dried beans. Instruct the teams to open the bags and sort the beans by type. Explain to them that the first group that separates their bag of beans correctly will win a prize! (Make the prize something that students will really want to work for, e.g., a free assignment pass, first in line for lunch for one week, etc.)

3. Listen carefully to the conversations of each group as the activity progresses. Notice how other members of each team handle the plant's disagreement with what the team wants to do. Do they disagree appropriately and find a way to work together? You will find that some groups will work as a team while others will separate, work alone and then add their work together at the end. This activity will give you a good idea of the teamwork capability of your students. To win, they must find a way to work through disagreement, work fast, and work together.

4. At the end of the activity, hold a class discussion. **Do not reveal who the plants are** prior to answering these questions:

   • How did it make you feel when your group started to argue?

   • Did your group use the social skills of accepting "No" for an answer and disagreeing the right way correctly?

   • Could your group have done a better job using those skills with one another? If so, how?

5. Reveal the "plants" to the rest of your class and discuss their role in the activity.

6. Announce the winning team and award their prize!

You Be the Author!

Teacher Instructions

1. Read the book *"I Just Don't Like the Sound of No!"* to your students.

2. Then ask the students to rewrite the story (or a part of the story) so that RJ is never told "No" and is always told "Yes."

3. Have your students answer the following questions:

- What would your life be like if, every time you asked your parents to buy you something, they did?

- What would your life be like if you were allowed to have sleepovers any time you wanted to?

- What would your life be like if your teacher let you have free time anytime you asked for it?

- Do you think that sometimes being told "No" is a good thing or a bad thing? Explain.

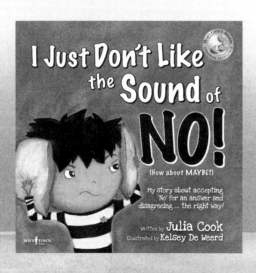

Say YES to NO Club T-Shirt!

Teacher Instructions

Distribute the handout with the outline of a T-shirt from the CD-ROM. The handout includes the following student instructions.

Student Instructions

As an official member of the "Say Yes to No!" club, you have been given the task of designing the new club T-shirt! Use the T-shirt outline below to create your design. Have fun! Be creative!!!

Yes, Yes, NO Tag!

OBJECTIVE
Help students learn social skills from sharing and discussing their classmates' experiences. This activity is most appropriate for grades preK-1.

Teacher Instructions

1. Have your students sit in a circle facing inward.

2. Designate one student to begin the game by being "It." The student should walk around the circle and tap the other students' heads saying "Yes" several times until he taps someone and says "No."

3. The student who is tapped with a "No" should get up, chase and try to tag the person who is "It" around the circle.

4. The goal is for the "No" student to tag the "It" classmate before he is able to sit down in the "No" student's spot. If the "No" student is not able to do this, he becomes "It" for the next round and play continues.

5. If the student who is "It" is tagged, he should sit in the center of the circle and tell about a time when he was told "No" for an answer. Have the students briefly discuss how using the skills of disagreeing appropriately and accepting "No" for an answer could be used in the situation just described.

6. Ask another student to be "It" for the next round. The student in the middle of the circle cannot leave until another student is tagged to replace him.

The Answer Is NO!

OBJECTIVE
This activity offers students opportunities to practice accepting "No" for an answer, even when the "No" may be unreasonable.

Teacher Instructions

1. Begin the day as usual, however, whenever your students ask you a "yes or no" question, respond by saying NO! (Exception: When a child asks to use the restroom.) It won't take long before your students realize that they are being told "No" in response to every request.

2. At the end of the activity, verbally praise students who accepted the "No" appropriately and discuss the following questions as a group:

   - How did it make you feel when I continually said "No" to you?
   - Was it hard not to argue?
   - Why do you think we did this activity?

Life without 'No'

Teacher Instructions

1. Hand out the activity sheet included on the CD-ROM and ask students to imagine what life would be like if they were never told "No." Ask them to list the advantages and disadvantages of sometimes being told "No."

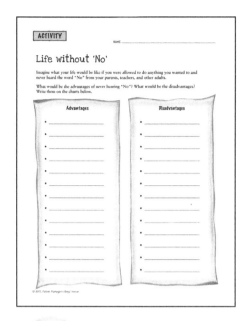

2. Draw a chart on your classroom white- or blackboard that is similar to the one on the activity sheet. Ask students to give you the advantages and disadvantages from their activity sheets to write on the board.

3. When the lists are finished, ask your class the following questions:

- Did you list more advantages or disadvantages?

- Do you think the advantages of sometimes being told "No" outweigh the disadvantages or not? Explain.

Activity Extension

Have students draw a picture of what they and their family or friends would look like if they were never told "No." See if they can include picturing some of the advantages and disadvantages they listed on their activity sheet.

19

My Favorite Is

OBJECTIVE

This activity helps students practice the skill of disagreeing appropriately by respectfully debating their choices for favorite things.

Teacher Instructions

1. Pass out the *My Favorites* activity sheet (also on the CD-ROM) and have each student fill it out.

2. Tally the results and find the favorites for each question by selecting the two answers with the most student "votes." Write both of the favorites for each question on the board.

   EXAMPLE: Favorite flavor of ice cream is … Strawberry/Chocolate

3. Ask students to raise their hand if they think that strawberry ice cream is better than chocolate. Choose one student that agrees with the statement and one student who disagrees and have them come to the front of the room. Have the student who thinks that strawberry is better than chocolate voice his or her opinion and the reasons for that opinion.

4. As a class, review the steps for disagreeing appropriately:

   Look right at the person when you disagree.
   Don't scream or use mean words, be the best you can be.
   Tell why you feel differently, give your reasons with facts.
   Listen closely to what she says, this is how you should act.

5. Now ask the student who disagrees with the statement model those social skill steps as he or she responds to the first student's comments. Have the two students continue to debate their conflict while modeling the skill steps.

6. Repeat with additional favorites until some or most of the topics have been discussed.

7. Discuss the following question as a class:
   Why is it important to use the skill steps when you disagree with someone?

ANSWERS MIGHT INCLUDE:

It might keep people from getting into fights. You can avoid making a person feel bad. You can show respect for others. You can avoid making a person feel angry. You can figure out how to agree to disagree.

NAME _____

My Favorites

Write down your very favorite . . .

Flavor of ice cream:
_____

Movie:
_____

Book:
_____

Color:
_____

Fruit:
_____

Candy:
_____

Animal:
_____

Day of the Week:
_____

Month of the Year:
_____

Professional Athlete:
_____

Car:
_____

Smell:
_____

Beverage:
_____

Food:
_____

Time of Day:
_____

Type of Music:
_____

Season of the Year:
_____

BeaNO!

Materials Needed

🦕 Two flavors of jelly beans

🦕 Small sample cups, one for each student, containing one or two beans of each flavor

I REALLY DON'T LIKE THE TASTE OF JELLY BEANS.

MY PARENTS HAVE TOLD ME NOT TO EAT SWEETS AT SCHOOL.

Teacher Instructions

1. Prior to this activity, pull one student aside privately and explain that he or she must say "No" to eating the jelly beans you will offer to the class. (NOTE: Select this student very carefully and purposefully. This activity is best done with older children when you have a student who will be able to resist the peer pressure for a few minutes without becoming flustered or emotional.) Review the steps to disagreeing appropriately with the student. You can provide the student with some reasons why he or she would refuse to eat the jelly beans: "My parents have told me not to eat sweets at school; I really don't like the taste of jelly beans, etc."

2. Explain to your students that you would like all of them to taste two different flavors of jelly beans. Tell them that you are participating in a test-market survey for a brand of jelly beans and if you can get your entire class to sample them and comment on their flavor via the company's Website by 10 a.m. (time may be adjusted as needed) you could win one hundred dollars.

3. When the selected student doesn't eat the beans, ask him why. Begin to persuade him or her to taste the jelly bean. Offer class rewards (extra recess, free assignment passes, etc.) for tasting the bean. Tell students that you have already submitted your class roster and all students must participate for you to win.

4. Students will begin to apply peer pressure. When this happens, up the stakes even more by telling your students that you will give them the hundred dollars to buy something special for your classroom.

5. When arguments start to arise, listen for students who can disagree appropriately and/or accept the student's "No" response for an answer.

6. After a few minutes, tell the truth about the activity, praise the students who used the skills correctly, and have a follow-up discussion asking these questions:

   • How did you feel when _____ said "No" to eating the jelly beans?

   • Did you disagree appropriately? Did the other student disagree with you appropriately?

   • How can peer pressure affect your decision making?

   • How will this activity help you when you are in a situation where you need to say "No" (e.g., when you are offered drugs or alcohol, etc.)?

Rap It Up!

Teacher Instructions

1. Divide your class into groups of five to six students each.

2. Have each group compose a rap based on one of the social skills. They can use the skill poems from *I Just Don't Like the Sound of NO!* or start from just the basic steps, both of which are given below:

To accept "No" for an answer, this is what you need to do:

Look right at the person who is telling you "No."

Say "Okay" to the person, he's running the show.

Stay calm on the inside and don't disagree.

You can ask him why later, this is how you should be.

To disagree with someone the right way, here is what you should do:

Look right at the person when you disagree.

Don't scream or use mean words, be the best you can be.

Tell why you feel differently, give your reasons with facts.

Listen closely to what she says, this is how you should act.

Accepting "No" Skill Steps

Look at the person.

Say "Okay."

Stay calm and don't argue.

Ask why later.

Disagreeing Appropriately Skills Steps

Look at the person.

Use a pleasant voice.

Tell why you feel differently and your reason.

Listen to the other person.

3. Have students perform their raps in front of each other and in front of other classes.

It's Game Time!

Materials Needed

🦕 Poster Board, Construction Paper

🦕 Rulers, Scissors, Paste, Other Art Supplies

🦕 Crayons or Markers

🦕 Plastic Checkers or Poker Chips (to use as tokens)

Teacher Instructions

1. Have students work in groups of four to five and design a game and game board around mastering the social skill steps of accepting "No" for an answer and disagreeing appropriately. The concept of the game could be to acquire eight cards (each with one of the following skill steps written on it) and place them in the correct order. Make sure you have several board games in your classroom that students can view as examples, e.g., Chutes and Ladders, LIFE, Monopoly, etc.

2. Have students play the games they have created throughout the school year.

ACCEPTING "NO" FOR AN ANSWER

Look right at the person who is telling you "No."

Say "Okay" to the person, he's running the show.

Stay calm on the inside and don't disagree.

You can ask him why later, this is how you should be.

DISAGREEING THE RIGHT WAY

Look right at the person when you disagree.

Don't scream or use mean words, be the best you can be.

Tell why you feel differently, give your reasons with facts.

Listen closely to what she says, this is how you should act.

Disagreements All Around Us!

OBJECTIVE

Help students notice that disagreements occur around them and out in society all the time. This activity will get them to notice how well people handle disagreements at many levels.

Teacher Instructions

1. Make copies of the *Disagreements All Around Us* activity sheet on the CD-ROM for your students.

2. Ask them to spend a few days taking notice of how people close to them (family, friends, neighbors) and people in the news (citizens and/or officials in their city, state, country or the world) handle disagreements both appropriately and inappropriately. Tell students they may use personal examples or examples from history and articles from their local newspaper, TV news shows, or Internet news sites (if appropriate for your grade level).

3. Hand out the activity sheets and assign a completion date.

4. When the activity sheets are turned in, have a class discussion that addresses what students learned about how people disagree and resolve their differences.

Here are some examples of what students may report on their activity sheets.

IN MY HOME: arguing with my sister over what program to watch on TV; deciding what movie the family should watch together

IN MY CLASSROOM: pushing to be first in line for recess or lunch; figuring out how to take turns using the classroom computer

IN MY NEIGHBORHOOD: yelling at a baseball umpire over a call; neighbors calmly discussing what to do about a barking dog

IN MY TOWN OR CITY: a fight that results in the police being called; city or town council members debating a budget proposal

IN MY STATE: protesters vandalizing the state capitol; people holding a peaceful protest at the state capitol

IN MY COUNTRY: the Civil War; Democrats and Republicans in the U.S. Congress reaching a compromise over proposed legislation

IN THE WORLD: war; formation of the United Nations

ACTIVITY

Being the BEST at Accepting 'No'

Think about how improving your skill at accepting "No" for an answer could help improve your life. Answer these questions in two or three sentences.

How could accepting "No" for an answer the right way help you at home? Explain. _____

_____

_____

_____

_____

How could accepting "No" for an answer the right way help you at school? Explain. _____

_____

_____

_____

_____

Think of another place in your life where accepting "No" for an answer the right way could help you.

Explain. _____

_____

_____

_____

How could accepting "No" for an answer the right way help you later on when you have a job?

Explain. _____

_____

_____

Being the BEST at Disagreeing

Think about how improving your skill at disagreeing the right way could help improve your life. Answer these questions in two or three sentences.

How could disagreeing with someone the right way help you at home? Explain. _____

_____

_____

_____

_____

How could disagreeing with someone the right way help you at school? Explain. _____

_____

_____

_____

_____

How could disagreeing the right way help you when you are with your friends? Explain. _____

_____

_____

_____

How could disagreeing with someone the right way help you later on when you have a job? Explain.

_____

_____

_____

_____

Disagreeing Appropriately: Let's Look at the Past

Interview a grown-up (parent, grandparent, neighbor, or friend) by asking them the following questions. Write down their answers.

Can you describe a time in your life when you were younger that you had a strong disagreement with

someone? Explain. _____

_____

_____

_____

_____

Did you end up having an argument? _____

_____

_____

_____

_____

_____

How did this experience affect your relationship with this person or your life? _____

_____

_____

_____

_____

_____

Looking back now, should you have done things differently? _____

_____

_____

_____

_____

_____

_____

_____

What did you learn from this experience? _____

_____

_____

_____

_____

_____

_____

_____

What advice do you have for me now about handling disagreements? _____

_____

_____

_____

_____

_____

Who's the Boss?

Teacher Instructions

1. Make copies of the *Who's the Boss?* activity sheet on the CD-ROM.

    Activity sheet questions are:

    - Describe a time when a decision was made for you that you did not agree with.

    - Who made the decision for you?

    - How did it make you feel?

    - When you did not get your way, what did you do?

    - What do you think the person's reason was for making the decision for you?

    - Looking back, do you think the decision was the right one? Why or why not?

    - If you were in that person's shoes, how would you have handled the decision?

    - Why is it important for you to be able to accept decisions made by people in authority?

2. Have a short discussion with students about how parents, teachers, coaches, and other adults often make decisions for them.

3. Explain that this activity sheet asks them to think about a time when someone made a decision they did not agree with and to answer questions about what happened, how they felt, and how they handled it.

4. Distribute the activity sheets as an in-class or homework assignment.

5. After the activity sheets have been completed, have a follow-up discussion about what they learned by thinking about this topic. Ask them to describe the best way(s) to handle decisions made by people in authority.

If the Only Answer Was...

> **OBJECTIVE**
> This activity gets children thinking about how chaotic their classroom would be if they were allowed to do anything they wanted and asked for. On the other hand, if students and teachers only said "No" to each other, nothing would get done in a classroom that would probably be a pretty unhappy place.

Teacher Instructions

1. Ask students to brainstorm about what your classroom would be like if every time a student asked a question, your answer was "Yes."

2. After the brainstorm session, ask students to draw a picture of their "Yes-Only Classroom."

3. Now ask students to brainstorm about what your classroom would be like if every time a student or teacher asked a question, the answer was "No."

4. After the brainstorm session, ask students to draw a picture of their "No-Only Classroom."

5. Have students compare their two pictures and then draw a picture of a "Perfect Classroom."

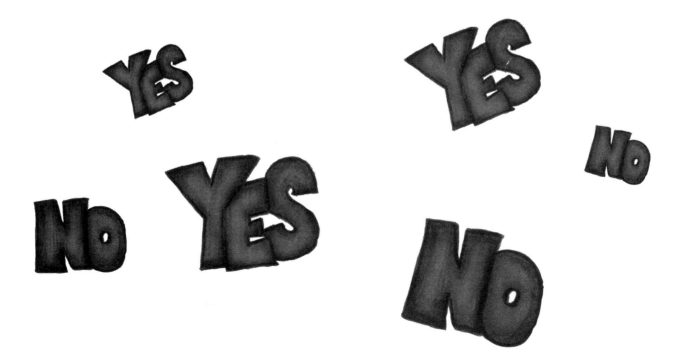

'Yes' or 'No' for a Day!

Teacher Instructions

1. Have students keep a tally of each time they hear someone say the word "Yes" during the course of one day. Tell them to try to include every "Yes" they hear, including at home, in the classroom, on the playground and school bus, on a TV program, etc.

2. On a subsequent day, have students keep a tally of each time they hear someone say the word "No" during the course of one day. Tell them again to try to include every "No" they hear, including at home, in the classroom, etc.

3. After two days of tallying, have students answer the following questions:

   • Did you tally more "No" answers or more "Yes" answers?

   • How big was the difference in the two tallies?

   • If there was a big difference, why do you think that occurred?

   • Do you think these tallies would be the same on most days?

   • Do the tallies tell us anything about the importance of accepting "No" for an answer?

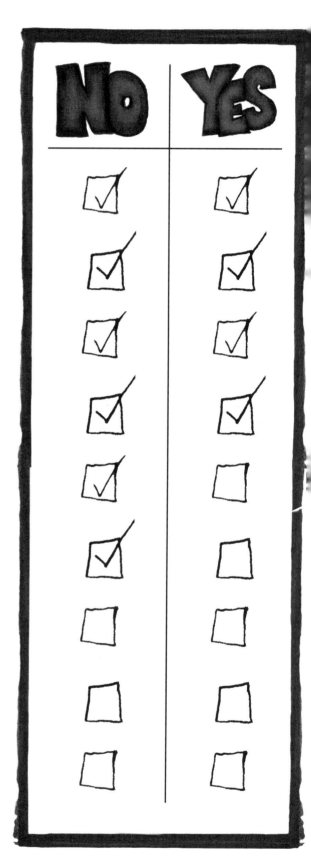